© Emmaline Severn 2023
All rights reserved

ISBN 9781738556830

Lost Voices Publishing
www.the-field-detectives.com

All characters appearing in this work are fictitious. Any resemblance to real persons, living or dead, is purely coincidental.

I dedicate this story to my amazing Dad, whom I miss every day, and to all those who bravely risked and lost their lives to serve in WWII.

Preface

The First World War was supposed to be the war to end all wars. Nevertheless, twenty-one years later, the world was drawn into a second bloody and savage conflict. Very few families were shielded from death and brutality, and my family in Nottinghamshire were no exception. Fear - and worse - stalked them for almost six years as Britain and its allies fought Nazi Germany and Japan to the bitter end. For eighteen-year-old Ted, who joined the Royal Navy as a medic and wanted to preserve life, it was a journey into the unknown, with the threat of death a constant companion. Yet he didn't dwell on the dark side of life, enjoying himself as much as he could before the D-Day landings of 1944, and the liberation of Europe began.

Introduction

Battleships, Destroyers, Frigates, and Aircraft Carriers; everyone has heard of them, but what about Landing Ship Tanks, known as LSTs?

They were huge, flat-bottom ships that were designed during WWII to transport tanks, equipment, supplies and soldiers to just about anywhere in the war-torn world of 1939-1945. Their development went a long way in helping the Allied victory.

Among the crew of the LSTs and other vessels were Sick Berth Attendants, (SBA) the 'medic' aboard ship. They were responsible for the health and well-being of the ship's company and continue to serve in the Royal Navy today.

"STEADY AS SHE GOES"

The poignant wartime recollections of a WWII Navy 'medic'.

'Hi Dad, how are you today?' I walked toward the man whose love, compassion and strong moral compass had guided me all my life and planted a big kiss on his cheek.

'Oh, you know me, love, I can't complain, just old age and poverty,' he replied.

His charismatic smile lit up an old, wise face, a face I loved. He was eighty-six years old and unwell now, his weary heart was failing, but his mind was still sharp. At my visit last week, as part of my family history research, he'd promised to tell me more about his navy days when he was a medic, or Sick Berth Attendant to give him his correct title, during the second world war. He always told the funny stories, but this time I asked him to talk about the real stuff.

'Here's your cuppa, Ted,' a voice I recognised said.

It was my husband. He placed the teacup and a plate of biscuits on the little wicker table at the side of Dad's comfy armchair. He loved my Dad too, in fact, everyone did, he was just one of those blokes. Dad reached over, picked up the cup with a shaky hand, blew on it and took a big, noisy slurp. I cast a smile at Richard, who was trying to keep a straight face and now had pen and paper ready to write down everything I hoped Dad would reveal.

I let him settle and brush the Digestive crumbs off the brown, woolly cardigan he always wore.

'Messy bugger,' he muttered to himself. 'Right, where did we get to last time?'

'Pass me the note-pad, Richard,' I said and looked at what he'd jotted down from the week before. 'Well, we got as far as you teasing me that those LSTs you were on were called large, slow targets, and I fell for it!'

Dad's roguish sense of humour had earned him the gift of a gigantic wooden spoon one Father's Day, which still hung on a hook in the back porch. He could always stir up a story and pull you in without you even realising it.

'They were,' Dad replied while trying to keep a straight face. 'Their real name might have been Landing Ship Tanks, but large, slow targets they flippin' well were! Especially when they were fully loaded up with tanks, men and equipment. They were the forerunners of the drive-on, drive-off ferries we have nowadays, you know.'

'You also need to tell me more about those nurses, the VADs, what was it you called them?'

'Virgins Awaiting Destruction!'

'Honestly Dad, that's terrible. You'd never get away with that nowadays, you know!'

Dad chuckled. 'Mind you, there were one or two of them whose destruction had already taken place, and they had a bad reputation. Nothing to do with me though!'

I looked at Dad who had an angelic look on his face, which made me burst out laughing.

'What about the woman, Rose, who played the piano in the pub you used to go to on Union Street?' I asked.

Dad's face broke into such a smirk, and I knew that this was definitely one of his tales we needed to get down.

'Did I tell you about when the captain came back aboard worse for drink, tripped up and sprained his ankle?' he asked.

'Yes Dad, that's one of your favourites. You told us you had to strap it up and swear never to tell anyone. Did you?'

Tapping the side of his nose, he said, 'Well, that'd be telling, wouldn't it?'

He took another slurp of his tea.

'How about we start from the beginning, Dad? The night you came home to find your call-up papers had arrived.'

His grey-brown eyes misted over as memories of bygone days returned…

A pea-souper swirled in the night sky as Ted wearily made his way home from a long shift at the hosiery factory where he spent his working life knitting stockings. Ten hours a day running back and forth, attending to the clattering machines was tough, but Ted's happy-go-lucky nature, and ability to turn his hand to anything, meant he took everything in his stride. It helped that the pay was good too. As he walked down the steep hill to his home in Nottingham, he lit a Players Navy Cut and inhaled deeply, pulling his coat collar up around his neck in a valiant attempt to keep the cold at bay.

'I hope Mum's feeling better,' he whispered to himself. 'That last letter from our Jack didn't half upset her.'

Ted's elder brother had been taken prisoner by the Germans and was being held as a POW at a camp in Annaburg. Their mother was trying bravely to keep herself together. Still, Ted knew she cried herself to sleep at night as he could hear her through the thin wall that separated the bedrooms in their small council house.

It was nearly 11 o'clock when he arrived home, and to his surprise, a light was still on in the front room. His Mum and Dad never stayed up much after ten, what had happened, Ted wondered. He unlocked the front door, stepped into the hallway, prised off his shoes, and hung his grey gaberdine mac on the wall pegs.

'Is that you, our Ted?' Stan's voice called out.

'Yes, Dad, who else is it going to be?' The reply was meant to be funny, but Ted stopped in his tracks when he heard sobs arising from the other room. It was Pat.

Ted pushed open the door to find his dad comforting her on the settee, she held a soggy handkerchief in her hands and looked like she'd been crying for quite some time.

'What's up? What's happened? Why are you crying, Mum?' Ted's mind was in overdrive.

'This arrived in the post today.' Stan passed his youngest son a letter; it was his call-up papers.

Pat looked up, and Ted could see her red-rimmed eyes. 'I don't want you to go, Ted,' she sniffed, 'I lost our Harold, Jack's a prisoner, and now they've come for you. It's not fair. Haven't they taken enough from us?' She began to cry again.

All three of them knew this day would come. Ted had turned eighteen in the summer, and it was inevitable he would be called up soon after; there was nothing anyone could do. He'd chosen the Royal Navy instead of a squaddie life as he had no ambition to become cannon fodder. So, last year with his best mate, Jim, they'd joined the British Red Cross and trained as first aiders, standing them in good stead for when they were called up. Once a week, they attended overnight air raid duty to be on hand if any injuries occurred, and Ted was proud to be doing something for the war effort.

When his brother died five years ago, Ted had watched in awe at the hospital as a doctor tried to save him. Had he come from a wealthy background, he would have studied medicine. However, a framework knitter's son didn't stand a chance of becoming a doctor, so a Sick Berth Attendant would be the closest thing he could ever hope for, and he'd be able to sail the seas. The sight and smell of the sea were rarely an option for a young man from the Midlands, except if the family could rustle up enough money for a week in a Skegness boarding house. Even then, the brown, dirty-looking North Sea was never very inviting, not even for rolled-up trouser leg paddling.

He sat down on the settee next to his distraught mother and put his arm around her. She was a quiet, pretty, gentle soul, and although her complexion was smooth and fresh, the grey streaks in her hair betrayed her age. Now in her fifties, terrible memories of losing two brothers in the first world war, added to the continuing death and devastation in this one, had finally taken its toll on her nerves.

'I'll be all right, Mum, you know me. I've no intention of getting shot or captured, I'll be aboard ship to make people better. It's just as important, and I get the chance to practice my first aid for real.'

Ted tried his best to reassure his mother despite his stomach churning with his own anxiety. Even in the navy, there was still a very realistic prospect of being torpedoed or bombed, and he was trying his utmost to keep the bag of chips he'd eaten on the way home from work from depositing themselves on the front room carpet.

Stan was relieved Ted had chosen the navy rather than the army as he'd done in the Great War. Stationed at one of the general hospitals in France, he'd been a private in the RAMC Cycling Corps. The gnarled tapestry of varicose veins in his legs, caused by a life of tending knitting machines six days a week, had prevented him from being sent to the trenches.

'Thanks for small mercies,' he exclaimed to himself the day he was conscripted.

Despite this good fortune, Stan would still witness his share of horrors. The bombing of their hospital being one of the worst, and the appalling injuries he saw were just for starters. Rough and ready, but with a heart of gold, he certainly wasn't going to lose another son; he knew it would finish Pat if they did.

Ted had a few days to pack and say his goodbyes, and after his last morning shift at the factory, Jim insisted on a pub crawl that evening around town to remind them of home. Jim's call-up papers were due in the next few weeks, and the two friends silently wondered if they would ever see each other again.

'Come on, Ted, one last pint at the Salutation,' Jim slurred.

'Aye, Aye Cap'n. Bar ahoy,' Ted joked.

They pushed their way through the packed pub, full of soldiers home on leave. The smell of tobacco smoke, spilt beer and the bellowing of laughter from a group of soldiers in the corner had created a cheerful atmosphere. You could sense the relief that the men had survived and made it home for a while before they were forced to live through the next carnage.

'Two pints of Mackeson, please.' Ted was six feet tall and thin as a rake, so his height enabled him to lean over the slight young woman standing patiently at the bar waiting to be served and get in first with his drinks order.

'Oy! Who do you think you are, pushing in front like that?' The pretty brunette flashed her dark brown eyes at Ted as she spoke.

'Beg your pardon, me lady, I didn't see you down there.' Ted quipped.

'So, you're a comedian, are you - and a rude one at that?'

'I do have my moments, so I'm told.'

'I don't think this is one of them!'

Ted continued to look down at the girl, who was about seventeen years old and bristling with anger.

'I've been standing here for ten minutes trying to get served, and here you are all lofty, getting served before me. Well, you'd better add two port and lemons to your order for me and Cynthia over there.'

Firmly put in his place, Ted did as he was told. Carrying the drinks, he precariously made his way to the round, wooden table where Cynthia was sitting and already being charmed by Jim. The four young people sat together for an hour or so, the girls laughing at Ted's terrible jokes. Still, there was an underlying tenseness, as they all knew that Ted's life would change forever when morning broke.

Ted woke, rubbed his eyes and massaged the sides of his head, which were pounding relentlessly. 'Serves me right,' he thought to himself, 'but it's probably the last pint I'll have for a while.'

It was the 30th of November 1943, and soon a train would be waiting to take him to HMS Glendower, the recruitment assessment camp in Pwllheli.

Breakfast was a subdued affair. Afterwards, Ted stood in the hallway clutching his battered, brown leather suitcase, he looked at his mum and dad, gulped back his emotions and said his goodbyes. Pat cried as her son circled his long arms around her and squeezed her tight.

'Love you, Mum. I'll write as often as possible. I'll be back as soon as we've sorted that Hitler bloke!'

Then he looked to his left and swore he could see a tear welling in his father's eyes too, but he blinked it away as he imparted some words of wisdom.

'Keep your head down, and volunteer for now't! Eat everything that's put in front of you, and if some bugger pinches any of your stuff, pinch some bugger else's.' These were some of the essential lessons learned from Stan's days in the RAMC.

It was bitterly cold, and the sharp northeast wind blowing in Ted's face seemed to press him back as if it were trying to prevent him from reaching the tram stop. But, get there he did, and he set his suitcase down on the pavement so he could light a cigarette.

He entered Midland Station, which was heaving with servicemen either leaving or arriving home. Women were waving, and others were crying, most with children hanging on their coats, having no idea what was happening. Ted pushed his way through the crowd to platform three, where a train stood patiently belching steam and smoke everywhere. He managed to find a window seat and hoisted his suitcase onto the overhead rack. A cocktail of emotions rippled through Ted's mind as the train pulled out of the station. He watched as the smoky chimneys of Nottingham disappeared into the distance, and a feeling of loneliness crept over him. His life at the factory, his mates at the pub, and his mum and dad – these were all he knew.

'Are you headed for boot camp?'

Ted's thoughts were interrupted quite suddenly by the voice of the young man sitting in the seat opposite.

'Uh, what, oh yes,' he stuttered. 'I'm headed for Wales, are you?'

'Yes, HMS Glendower. Did you know it used to be a Butlins holiday camp? It's not going to be much of a holiday for us, is it?' the man said.

He was about Ted's age, with a shock of ginger hair, freckles and a friendly smile. 'Sid Bates. But my mates call me Rusty.'

'Ted Hilton.'

Rusty held out a pack of Navy Cuts, and Ted took one. They both lit up and drew deeply. The two 'sailors to be' in the adjacent seats had nodded off. One of them was snoring, almost in time with the clackety-clack of the train, as its wheels sped along the tracks.

'I thought Glendower was a ship! Any idea what happens when we get there?' Ted asked.

'Loads of square-bashing, I suppose.' Rusty replied.

'Oh well, we'll soon find out when we get there. I hope the snaps good!'

They sat and chatted about where they were going after the initial training. Rusty had a yearning for the high seas after reading Treasure Island as a kid. He told Ted this would be a chance to escape his tedious job at the hardware shop and breathe some fresh sea air. Ted talked about his own ambitions.

The journey to Pwllheli took an age. Ted could only catnap on the train, so he arrived with the rest of the newly enlisted men, tired and hungry. It was perishingly cold as dawn approached. They'd been picked up by naval transport at the train station and dropped off at HMS Glendower, where a multitude of bewildered and apprehensive young men walked through the iron entry gates and was led to the reception area by the voice of a ghostly petty officer that boomed out from a hidden tannoy. Ted suddenly wanted to go home but knew that was impossible, he was here for the stay. He swallowed, squared his shoulders and looked around him. The lad at his side was visibly trembling, and he looked as if he hadn't even started shaving. Over the heads of most of the long line of men, Ted could see a table where three officers were checking in the latest round of recruits and directing them to their chalets.

With four sets of bunk beds per chalet, space was rather tight. Ted bagged a top bunk, which was a good call because, after only a couple of hours of sleep, the blaring sound of a bugler made them jump from their skins at six o'clock in the morning.

The shocked and dazed voice of the occupant beneath Ted called out: 'Flippin Eck. What's that racket?'

Ted leaned over to see the chap below and saw a shock of ginger hair with a hand massaging his head. He had just smacked his head against Ted's bunk. It was Rusty. Smiles broke out on both their faces as they recognised one another as they'd hit it off on the train. And if the sound of reveille at the crack of dawn didn't jolt them from their sleep, a blasting voice over the tannoy most certainly did.

'All men are to report to the clothing store in fifteen minutes.'

'This is it, lads, looks like we're in the navy now,' Ted said as he swung his legs off his bunk and jumped down. In unison, they all hurried to wash, shave and dress before they were led away to be kitted out, after which they were subjected to a medical, the dentist and given inoculations…

'You must have been shattered, Dad,' I said.
'Well, you had it to do, nothing more to it,' he replied.

'So, what did they kit you out with?'

'Well... there was a great big khaki kit bag for starters, and the uniform was a blue jacket and trousers, with a white shirt and black tie, and what with the peaked cap and black boots, I looked more like a railway porter. In fact, I was once stopped on a platform and asked what time the next train to London was.'

The comment led to a bout of laughter. Once we had cleared our throats and regained our composure, I asked Dad what the training involved. He talked about learning basic naval training and how to march. He even fired a gun.

'We had to lay down on our bellies and aim at the target. I remember they kept telling us to 'shoot to kill'. We only had a few attempts, and I wasn't the best shot and really hoped I'd never have to shoot anyone. And we also had to learn to row...

'Right, men. Today is rowing training, but due to the inclement English weather, it's too dangerous to go out to sea, so a simulation has been set up at the outdoor swimming pool.' The voice belonged to Petty Officer Jarvis, and if he was impressed by the quality of his latest batch of recruits, he hid it well.

Ted sat in the training room listening with a slight sense of bemusement, imagining how they would row a boat in a swimming pool. He nudged Rusty in the arm and whispered, 'We shan't get very far. It's a good job Jerry won't be up our backsides.'

'I can't swim,' Rusty declared.

'Why did you join the navy then, you daft bugger?

'I didn't think we'd be rowing across the Channel!'

After the briefing, they filed out of the room and marched to the outside edge of the camp, where a huge swimming pool was situated. In it, a large rowing boat had been lowered into the pool and tethered at both ends. The first group of recruits climbed aboard the craft. It was rocking in the water courtesy of the gale that was blowing, giving them some idea of what it was like to be at sea. The crew took up their positions, and when they were ordered to do so, they began to pull on their oars.

Ted was rather impressed at the ingenuity of this simulation and waited in anticipation for his turn. A few men fell overboard, and by the end of the day, the group of cold, wet young men had experienced their first real taste of naval life…

'That's hilarious, Dad. I wish I could have seen it,' I said.

'They still do swimming pool rowing training now. The equipment's a bit snazzier, but the principal's the same. You row like mad but never get anywhere! We were quite ahead of the game in those days, you know.' he replied with a smug grin.

'So, where did you go after Butlins?'

'After that? Hmm, oh yes. That's when I first went to Plymouth. I spent about three weeks at Stonehouse Hospital while they decided what to do with us. I loved Plymouth. Some of my best memories were made there. Then it was off to Newton Abbot. There was me and about forty other blokes, and that's where I did my medical training. I had a head start because I'd done my first aid. Just a minute, I found my training manual to show you. We called it our bible; it had everything we needed to know, and we had to learn it all!'

With great effort, Dad pulled himself up from his chair and steadied himself. I jumped up to help him, but he smiled and said there was still life in the old sea dog yet. I knew it was an effort for him to move around, but he never complained and always laughed off his sluggishness. He made his way over to the sideboard, took a small blue book from one of the shelves, and sat back down in his chair, breathing heavily. 'Oooh, I'm buggered,' he said.

I took the book from him, the cover of which was now faded with age. I'd always been impressed with how Dad could bandage up a cut knee or a sprained ankle, I knew why now. I suspect, however, that the horrific injuries he must have witnessed would have required more than a bandage!

He also had a photograph of himself wearing a Red Cross uniform and standing with his brother just before he went off to the Middle East and was taken prisoner. They both looked so young, and I tried to imagine my seventeen-year-old grandson being drafted on his next birthday. The thought didn't bear thinking about.

Dad talked, explaining the depth of medical knowledge he was required to retain: anatomy, the bloodstream, different types of body tissues and cells; he had to know the human body almost as thoroughly as a doctor.

'They called us 'Doc' aboard ship.' Dad said. 'Only a ship with a company of a hundred or more would have a real doctor on board. On my ships, there was just me. It wasn't just about treating injuries and tying bandages, we had to know about diseases and how to treat them, I had to give them medicines and injections, and there was tons of paperwork. The training was very serious, and there wasn't much time for any fun, although I can remember us having a laugh practising artificial resuscitation.'

I listened intently to my dad, in awe of him.

'Have a look at the chapter on suffocation. We had to do that on each other, sitting on your partner's backs or fronts pushing their ribcage back and forth, it was knackering! I'm so pleased things have moved on since then, but I bet if push came to shove and there was no fancy equipment, those methods would still work.'

I found the pages Dad mentioned and couldn't believe what was depicted. The drawings and the procedures all looked so archaic. I made a mental note to show my daughter, who is a nurse, to see what she makes of it all.

Dad's training took six months. After that, he was sent off for two weeks to something called the Field Hygiene School.

'And do you know what?' he exclaimed. 'While I was there, some bugger nicked my knife and fork.'

'Did you follow Grandad's advice?' I asked.

''I most certainly did. I had my suspicions about who the culprit was; he was a right bully. So, I snook into his tent when he was at the lavvy and 'borrowed' his. It all evened out in the end because we had to hand all the cutlery back when the two weeks was up, and I went back to Stonehouse after this. Thankfully, I never saw that swine again.'

We couldn't help laughing, even if the subject of pilfering off each other wasn't the best of topics. But as Dad pointed out, it was survival, not a picnic…

The rays of May's early morning sunlight arrowed through the gaps in the thin curtains that barely met across the dormitory windows where Ted slept alongside three other newly qualified medics. For the next couple of months, his job was to care for the wounded, for it was time to put his training into action. The hospital layout impressed Ted. Built in the mid-18th century tradition as a naval hospital, it consisted of ten blocks arranged around a courtyard and designed in such a way as to help prevent the spread of infection. Colonnades linked the wards together, and Ted would move the patients to these areas for fresh air throughout the day. On Sundays, a brass band would play in the courtyard in an effort to boost morale. With his caring nature and intoxicating sense of humour, he developed a great rapport with the men. He also built up an excellent reputation with the medical teams and nursing staff.

For the time being, life wasn't too demanding, with enough free time to explore Plymouth and enjoy a pint or two on his evenings off.

'Are you up for a trip to Union Street tonight, Ted?' asked Arthur, with whom Ted had become quite good pals.

'I'm not sure, I've got my eye on Joan, that pretty VAD off my ward, and I was going to ask her out this evening,' Ted replied.

'A Virgin Awaiting Destruction, hey, Ted?'

'Joan's not like that, she's a nice girl. The VADs aren't all like Peggy, you know, who'll end up in trouble if she's not careful.'

Although Ted enjoyed a girl's company and might joke with the lads, he was far too much of a gentleman to take advantage of any of the nurses.

'Well, if Joan turns you down, you know where to find me,' Arthur said.

Sadly, Ted's offer for a drink at the Royal Sovereign was rebuked harshly by Joan. 'Who do you think I am? I wouldn't be seen dead with any of you Jack the lads! I've got my reputation to think of, you know.'

It seemed that all sailors were tarnished with the same brush, which left Ted extremely disappointed. Nevertheless, it was his evening off, so he decided to catch up with Arthur at the pub and enjoy a few pints with the lads. As he walked along the streets, the devastation caused by the blitz on Plymouth was evident all around. Most of the city had been reduced to rubble, killing over a thousand people and wounding thousands more. Ted passed the charred, skeletal ruin of Charles Church, another bleak reminder of why he was in Plymouth, and for a moment going for a pint seemed rather futile, knowing that sooner or later he would receive orders for his posting. Still, he continued walking, pressing these thoughts to the back of his mind.

The pub was packed solid. Tobacco smoke filled the

room, and above the sound of shouting and laughing, a piano could be heard with someone belting out *Roll Out the Barrel,* accompanied by a group of rowdy sailors. Ted manoeuvred his way through the crowd to the bar and ordered a pint of mild. He took a sip and licked the foam from his lips as he scoured the room for Arthur. His stature gave him a distinct advantage, and he soon spotted his pal standing alongside the sailors. Ted waved his arm hoping to attract his friend's attention.

'Ted, over here,' a voice could be heard above the din. As Ted gently pushed his way through the throng, the tightly packed room opened up. 'Joan turned you down then?' quipped Arthur.

'Afraid so. I don't think even my old mate Jim's charm could have thawed her. So, here I am. Blimey, it's busy in here tonight!'

It was difficult to make any conversation because of the din, so Ted lit a cigarette and took in his surroundings.

The pianist was a woman in her late thirties, wearing a burgundy swing dress with her brassy, bleached blonde hair pinned up in a coif. With stockings in such short supply for everyone, she had coloured her legs with tea and drawn a seam down the back with an eyebrow pencil. What more could a girl do in these hard times? She played a few songs and then stood up, squeezing herself between the piano and stool and turned around to face her audience who were at varying degrees of drunkenness. Her full lips were painted a deep, dark red, almost matching the colour of her dress, and her thinly plucked eyebrows were drawn into a high arch above her blue eyes. She smoothed the wrinkles from her dress and winked at a nearby matelot who quickly placed his pint glass on the sticky piano top alongside half a dozen others. The woman quietly slid through a side door that led to a small storeroom at the back of the pub, followed by the man. A few minutes later, he walked out with a satisfied grin on his face. The pianist resumed her place at the piano and began thumping out Don't Sit Under the Apple Tree.

Ted watched this scene with great interest and elbowed Arthur in the arm.

'Did you see that, Arthur?' he said.

'Who, Rose?' he replied, and Ted nodded. 'Evidently, she enhances her earnings round the back between tunes!'

The summer of 1944 was approaching, and rumours started spreading that an invasion of Normandy was on the cards, they were calling it D-Day. When Ted received orders to join the crew of his ship, he felt relieved – even strangely elated – that he could finally see some action.

An LST was over 300 feet in length, with a maximum

speed of only ten knots. They were developed to carry tanks, vehicles, cargo and men, and used landing craft to deposit them on the beach. Ted wrote a letter home relaying the news but, in reality, he could say very little. He tried not to imagine his Mum worrying and hoped his sister would keep her occupied with the arrival of her newborn grandchild. He also wrote to his friend, Jim, who had been drafted aboard another ship similar to his own, but smaller. Both men were bitterly disappointed at being split up for their training. They had been friends for many years and inseparable back home. Now they were unsure when or if they would see each other again.

Before long, Ted and his Stonehouse comrades found themselves on a train bound for Portsmouth, a city teeming with troops, tanks and munitions. Many thousands of soldiers were camped in the surrounding woods, ready to receive their final briefings before embarking on a journey that would condemn many to certain death. The view from Portsdown Hill was incredible. There were so many sea-going vessels that it looked as if you could walk across their decks from Portsmouth to the Isle of Wight. Ted's orders were to report to the captain of LST 423, and alongside the rest of the medical team, begin preparing the area that was to be used for treating casualties.

He stood on the quayside, watching on as tanks drove

through the gaping mouths of the bow doors of the LST, and onto its deck. Up to twenty Shermans, tanks used by the US army, could be accommodated on the ship as well as many infantry platoons.

Wearing a uniform that had the Geneva Cross pinned to his right arm, Ted stared up at the massive ship that was now his new home. He felt apprehensive as the sheer weight of responsibility that lay on his eighteen-year-old shoulders hit him hard. 'This is it,' he thought to himself. 'God knows what the next few weeks will bring?'

'Edward Hilton DMX 557745, reporting for duty, sir.' As he spoke, Ted gave the ship's captain his very best salute.

'Welcome aboard, Doc,' was the skipper's warm response.

Ted was followed up the gangplank in the same fashion by the men he would work closely with for the next few weeks, that is if they all survived the nightmare they were about to live.

Within a few days, a tented area at the back of the tank deck served as a temporary operating theatre. The rows of bunks would house the walking wounded, while the more serious injuries would be treated on the casualty's stretcher as he lay on the tank deck floor.

'I'm going on deck for a smoke, anyone coming?' Ted said, during a short break from their duties.

He was joined by Frank, an experienced medic who had taken Ted under his wing. The camaraderie among the crew was strong, knowing that if they worked together, life would be somewhat easier to bear.

Making their way up top, they passed by a metal grid, and Ted could see the tank deck gradually filling up. The upper platform was packed solid with trucks and equipment and not an inch of space remained anywhere. At the bow of the ship was a small area where soldiers and crew could loiter, talk to one another, and have a smoke, and that was where Ted and Frank were headed.

A dozen or so like-minded men were already enjoying the fresh air. Some were veteran sailors, others were new recruits like Ted, and each felt a sense of apprehension about the weeks ahead.

Everyone had carried out their duties efficiently and correctly, and the 'hospital' was as ready as it could ever be in anticipation of the horrendous injuries Ted knew would be inflicted on some of those on board the ship. His prayer was that it would be as few as possible.

Before the first rays of light had breached the dark clouds, thousands of Allied paratroopers landed behind the Normandy beaches. It was Tuesday, the 6th of June, and Operation Overlord had begun.

After departing Blighty, LST 423 ran alongside the battleships, cruisers, gunships and other vessels, in a column heading for France. So began a painfully slow journey across the Channel towards Sword Beach.

The LSTs laboured in the rough seas, and their flat-bottomed design made them quite unstable. With every wave, the ship's hull thumped down, and as its bow came up and the stern went down, the whole vessel shook. Ted was restless and worried the boat would come apart. Thankfully, he couldn't dwell on his thoughts, as soon, a long line of men had formed, all of them suffering from seasickness. There was very little he could give them, so the toilets were in constant use and everywhere reeked of vomit.

Ten hours in, they still hadn't reached France. Those left not reeling from seasickness lay quietly in their hammocks, each one contemplating their fates. Then it began.

'GENERAL QUARTERS,' bellowed a commanding voice over the ship's tannoy. 'All hands, man your battle stations.'

The boom, boom, boom of the battleships' guns became a constant deafening noise as the Allies bombarded the beaches and beyond, in an attempt to weaken some of the Nazi defences which would hopefully make it easier for the troops when they landed.

Ted went on deck and observed the soldiers of the 3rd British Infantry as they took their positions in the small landing crafts that had been lowered into the sea. Each man sat silently, knowing that when they arrived at the beach and the boat's ramp lowered, they would be running into the gates of hell. How many would return alive, no one knew…

'Dad, Dad, are you ok?' I asked. He'd stopped talking, and his eyes had misted over. I went over to him, kneeling down and taking his hands in mine.

'I'm sorry, I didn't want any of this to upset you. There's no need to carry on, we can do it another day.' I said tenderly.

Dad looked me in the eye and replied, 'No, it's alright, I want to tell you, I just need a minute. Put the kettle on, I could do with another cuppa.'

This was duly done, and after about half an hour, Ted felt ready to continue.

'Take your time, Dad. We've got all afternoon,' I said.

'I'm ok, all ship shape and Bristol fashion again. Where were we?' he asked.

'Could you see what happened to the soldiers from your ship?'

'No, we were anchored a few miles from shore. I do

remember all the ships around ours and the hundreds of barrage balloons above us. They helped stop the enemy planes from flying in low, but we were still in danger of being hit and blown up.'

'Were you scared?'

'Not at the time, everyone was high on adrenaline and waiting for the order to move in. It was afterwards that the nightmare started for me. Once the first wave of soldiers had secured the beaches, the landing craft beached, and then I did see the horror.'

He stopped for a moment to pull a tissue from the box on his table and wipe his runny nose.

'It had been carnage everywhere. Hundreds of men died, mown down by the German machine guns as they ran off the landing crafts. I'm glad I didn't see it happen, it was bad enough trying to treat the terrible injuries. Once the equipment was off the ship, the wounded were brought aboard. The field medics had done remarkable jobs at patching them up, and one of my jobs was to give them morphine shots. I had a bag full of needles and ampoules, and I just shut myself off, injecting them one after another. Time just stood still until they were all on board, and we were given the orders to return to England.'

I listened intently, finding it hard to believe what my dad was telling me.

'I don't know how you did it.' I said lamely.

'You just did,' he replied…

Above the incredible noise of tanks, trucks, and men shouting, Ted faintly heard a voice calling. 'Doc, Doc over here, quick. Bring your kit, this man needs help, now!'

He looked around to see where the voice was coming from and spotted a sergeant waving frantically as he stood amongst a row of injured men lying upon stretches on the deck floor. One of them had blood pouring from his leg. Ted hurried over and knelt down and immediately applied a tourniquet to the man's thigh in an effort to stem the flow. He cut away the now useless blood-soaked bandage. The sight of the wound made Ted's stomach turn, but he swallowed the bile acid that had risen in his throat and began tending to his patient, who was starting to lose consciousness. The exit wound from the bullet had turned the soft, wet, red flesh outwards, leaving a gaping hole, and he could see that the shattered tibia within had splintered and punctured the fibular artery. A fragment of bone must have moved when the soldier was carried aboard.

Ted worked quickly, applying iodine to the wound and surrounding skin. He asked the sergeant at his side to fetch him a bowl of water so he could wash his hands with Carbolic soap. The tourniquet was working, and Ted was able to tie a ligature around the artery, praying it would hold until a surgeon could see the man. He dressed the wound, gave him an injection of morphine and moved on to the next pitiful soul whose arm had been blown away when one of his squad stepped on a mine. Although he was the only survivor, it would be touch and go if he lived. Ted knew that these types of injuries nearly always became septic as fragments of shell and clothing stay embedded in the wound. He gave him a shot of morphine and sat by his side until its effects took hold.

Each casualty he tended to had either lost a limb or an eye or had their guts ripped open by machine gun fire. The injuries were sickening, and it was very doubtful if some of them would last the ten hours it would take to sail back to England.

On their return, the wounded were transported to various hospitals. Ted escorted a number of patients to Stonehouse. The soldier who lost his arm had died, septicaemia claiming him before a surgeon could get to work. Nothing could have been done for him other than to dose him up and keep him comfortable. It was the first death Ted witnessed. Alas, there would be many more.

Miraculously, the soldier with the ruined leg survived, and once they reached Stonehouse, he was whisked away for surgery. Ted assisted while the surgeon meticulously repaired the shattered bone using cheese wire to hold the fragments together.

Ted sat by his bedside, carefully monitoring his vital signs whilst he came round from the anaesthetic.

The man began to stir. 'Where am I?' he groaned.

'Good to have you back, Billy. You're in Stonehouse Hospital. You've had your leg fixed.' Ted replied. Billy attempted to sit up and winced with pain. 'It's alright. You'll not be going anywhere for a while, but you're still here. It was touch and go for a while.'

Billy looked at his leg dangling from the traction equipment above him.

'Don't suppose Tranmere will want me back with this gammy leg if this damned war ever ends.'

'You're a footballer?'

'I was, before the war.'

Well, that was it. Football dominated their conversation as Ted was an avid Nottingham Forest supporter. Before the war, he went with his Dad to every home match on a Saturday afternoon. It had been a ritual since Ted was a small boy that they caught a bus into town and walked down Drury Hill to Trent Bridge, where the Forest ground was situated. Maybe one day it would happen again, Ted thought to himself as he took Billy's temperature and changed the dressing on his leg.

When it was time for Ted to return to his ship, Billy had stirred and was in a much better place. Although he'd never be able to play football again, Ted's humour and compassion had helped Billy pull himself out from sliding into a dark place. He shook Ted's hand enthusiastically, thanking him for all he'd done.

'Steady as she goes, matey.' Ted said.

He never saw Billy again, but his medical records showed that he recovered from his injury and returned to his hometown, able to walk with a cane.

It wasn't long before Ted was back aboard the 423, which had now been turned into a hospital ship. A wardroom had been converted into an operating theatre, and the tank deck kitted out with long rows of stretchers spread three high against the walls and three deep on the floor. Tinned sardines had more room! More than a dozen trips were made back and forth across the Channel, to ferry the wounded back from France. Sleep for the crew was a premium – but the sacrifice was worth it, as about 40,000 men were rescued from the Normandy beaches in the weeks that followed the invasion…

We fell silent for a while, trying to take in what Dad had said whilst ensuring it was all written down. There was very little anyone could say after hearing all that, and when I felt

Dad was ready, I asked him what he did after D-Day.

'I had another stint at Stonehouse before I was drafted to the LST 3010. I think it was April 1945. We were off to the Far East, and before we left, I managed to get myself a doe-skin tiddly suit off the black market, it cost me £10. It was worth it though, I looked proper dapper.' He winked at me. 'Mind you, I've never told anyone this before, and it was well before I met your Mum, but that suit didn't half make a difference to Joan when I plucked up the courage to ask her out again!'

'Well, Mum was engaged to someone else before you remember, I never thought for a minute you hadn't had a girlfriend or two before her. It's okay,' I said.

'Once I'd wooed her with my charm and a few Babychams, we became quite close. She was my first real girlfriend, and I was very fond of her. We were only together for a few weeks, though.'

'Why, what happened?'

'It was awful. She was from London, and she went home on leave for a while and was run over by a bus and killed.'

'Oh, Dad. I'm so sorry.'

'It took a bit of getting over, I can tell you, but it was a long time ago, and if I hadn't met your mother, I wouldn't have you, would I?'

'I know, Dad, but that's so sad.'

'There was a great deal of sadness at that time. No one escaped death in some way or another, it was inevitable. But we all soldiered on, and soon after she died, I went off to the Far East...

A bitter war was being fought with the Japanese in the Far East, and Ted's ship was bound for Malaysia carrying troops and supplies. It was a long journey that would take weeks in an LST, and during this stretch, Ted was the only medic on board and when he embarked, he found the sick bay situated near the galley. A smile broke out on his face, as he didn't like being hungry. He set his kit bag on the floor of the small, white-painted, narrow room that was now his personal domain. To his right lay the examination bed with two overhead lamps. On the opposite wall, drawers and cupboards containing medical supplies filled the limited space. A small desk took centre stage, giving Ted the space he needed to sit and complete the paperwork that was appropriate to his duties. Meanwhile, at the far end was a sink with a mirror and the all-important poisons cabinet, to which Ted held the key.

For the next hour or so, he familiarised himself with the layout of the sick bay, carefully checking in each of the small drawers that were labelled with their contents; gauze, lint, various types of bandages, needles, syringes and a stock of Lysolats for disinfecting and sterilising. This new solid form of Lysol was now recognised as the most convenient and effective of all antiseptics. Ted was suitably impressed.

There was a tap on the door. 'There's a brew in the galley if you want one, Doc,' spoke a friendly voice.

Ted looked around to see a burly-looking steward with a welcoming smile on his face.

'I thought no one would ever ask,' Ted replied, grinning back.

'Albert Tomlinson at your service.'

'Ted Hilton.' The two men shook hands warmly.

Three further stewards were beavering away in the galley, cleaning the sinks and work areas and checking the food stocks, crockery, and cutlery. These men were vital to the smooth running of the ship. After all, a well-fed crew is nearly always a happy crew.

The layout of the ship was different from the 423 so Albert took Ted on a quick tour, showing him the shower area and toilets, the berthing deck where the hammocks were fastened three high to the walls. His height made sleeping in the hammocks very uncomfortable, so before long, his hammock was cast aside and sleeping on the examination bed took preference.

The ship was slow, and life was slow, but there was always the fear of being torpedoed or shelled by enemy aircraft. As they headed towards the Equator, the heat rose, and Ted treated many of the ship's company for sunburn. Fortunately, Ted was dark-skinned, and he was soon as brown as a berry and well settled into life at sea.

It was the evening of the 7th of May 1945, and while on deck, watching the ocean and smoking a cigarette, Ted was suddenly roused by the outbreak of a noisy commotion in another part of the ship. An excited young ensign came rushing up the steps shouting, 'The war is over, the war is over. Germany has surrendered! It's just come on the radio!'

Everyone began to cheer and throw their caps in the air after the captain confirmed the prime minister, Winston Churchill, would be delivering a speech at 3 o'clock British time the next day. Rum tots were given out early, with an extra one for good measure to celebrate the end of hostilities in Europe. Everyone felt enormous relief and celebrations lasted throughout the evening.

The following afternoon, Churchill's familiar voice spoke to the whole crew, who listened intently to every word.

'God bless you all. This is your victory! It is the victory of the cause of freedom in every land. In all our long history, we have never seen a greater day than this...'

It was a rousing speech, that also reminded everyone hostilities were still not over.

'There is another foe who occupies large portions of the British Empire, a foe stained with cruelty and greed - the Japanese. I rejoice we can all take a night off today and another day tomorrow.'

These words brought it home to Ted and the rest of the crew that despite the Allies' victory against the nazis, the LST 3010 was headed towards Japanese-occupied territory, where a potential nightmare scenario awaited them.

Their voyage continued, and after they'd been at sea for about four weeks, the ship docked at Cape Town. In the distance, Table Mountain dominated the view and evoked awe and amazement in everyone. The weather was beautiful, with azure skies and blistering sunshine, and that night most of the ship's company were granted shore leave.

That evening Ted and Albert set off with a group of matelots and headed off in the direction of the town. The delight of being able to walk around after so long at sea was liberating, and after stocking up on English cigarettes, visiting the cinema, and buying some food, they made their way to the bars. Some hours later, an extremely inebriated Ted staggered up the 3010's gangplank with Albert in tow. Somehow, he made it to his bed, only to be rudely awoken two hours later by a loud knock on the sick bay door.

'Doc, Doc. Wake up.' It was the petty officer. 'Doc, wake up. That's an order!'

'Bugger off!' Ted slurred.

Having been rudely awakened from his rather drunken sleep, Ted's unfortunate response was not met well. The Petty Officer opened the sick bay door with some force and demanded that Ted get up immediately and tend to a chap who'd injured himself on his return from shore. A somewhat subdued Ted returned to the sick bay an hour later, having lost his shore leave, his tot and was now at the beck and call of the Petty Officer whenever he required menial tasks to be carried out.

'That's a bit harsh,' Albert said when he enquired why Ted couldn't join him ashore that night.

'I know. It's not my fault some bugger fell down and hurt himself. At least I made it back to my bunk!' Ted grumbled, 'Seven days number elevens! We'll be back at sea by then. Trust me to open my big mouth.'

A couple of days later, his sick bay was visited by several men who had recently taken shore leave and were now experiencing some rather embarrassing itchiness. He had no choice but to arrange a full crew inspection. Up on deck, the men lined up and dropped their trousers and underpants as Ted checked each of the men's nether regions for lice. Those affected were ordered to shave the area, and a treatment of Unguentum Hydrargri was then well rubbed in. The whole procedure was undertaken with feigned dignity as most of the unaffected men were trying their best not to break out into roars of laughter.

Ted returned to the sick bay to write up his daily journal and medical notes, grateful there was a section on the various types of lice in his trusty medic's bible.

Back at sea, the 3010 lumbered its way eastward, and the days continued with the same routine until it was interrupted once more by the heart-stopping news that on the 6th and 9th of August, America had dropped two atomic bombs on Japan, killing and maiming over 200,000 people, mostly civilians. It was horrifying. The war with Japan was finally over, but the price paid was catastrophic. At first, the Japanese command in Singapore refused to accept the surrender, and they were willing to fight to the death, there was even a secret plan to massacre all Allied prisoners of war. In the end, they did surrender without any real resistance, but not before 300 Japanese officers and men committed hari-kari, and a platoon of soldiers blew themselves up with grenades.

On the 5th of September, the Allied fleet - consisting of hospital ships, landing craft and cargo ships - arrived in Singapore harbour, carrying food and medical supplies for the semi-starved population and released prisoners of war. Their duties now were to help restore Singapore and its people to some kind of normality. Ted treated as many of the sick as possible, most of whom were suffering from severe malnutrition, it was pitiful…

Once again, Ted's eyes glazed over as he remembered the skeletal people who had been starved and brutalised by war so long ago.

'You saw so much, Dad, you've never told me anything like this before, and you were so young,' I said, with a tear rolling down my cheek.

'Most of us were, but we shared the horror and the fun, and once you've got all this down in that book your writing, I only want to remember the fun parts again,' Dad replied.

'Nearly done. How did you get back home?' I asked.

'I was lucky. I'd have been stuck out there for months waiting for transport home, but another LST needed a medic, so I was drafted aboard and cadged a lift home on that. It was 1946 by the time I got back to England, and I was eventually demobbed at Plymouth. Believe me, I couldn't wait to get home. Your Grandma cried all day, and I never thought I'd feel so relieved to go back to my old job at the factory, I just wanted to put the war behind me.'

'Was Uncle Jack home when you got back?'

'Yes, he'd been freed while I was in the Far East, and me Mum was a bit miffed that he got married while I was still away. It didn't bother me. After everything he'd been through, he just wanted to marry your Aunty Doris and go back to his job. It was a terrible time, and I hope them flippin' politicians we've got these days never let it happen again!'

Richard finished writing the last sentence in the notebook, and we sat for a few minutes. I could see Dad was tired, reliving his experiences had taken a lot out of him, but as always, he never complained.

Ted died a few months later, and as I'd sat at the hospital bedside, holding his hand, I looked at his still handsome face and tried to flatten a curl of hair on his head.

'I love you, Dad,' I whispered. Don't leave me.'

He squeezed my hand. 'Don't worry, love, you'll be alright. I've had a good life…'

THE END

ACKNOWLEDGEMENTS

I would like to say a special, huge thank you to my friend and mentor, Tony Yorke, whose help and support with 'Steady As She Goes' are greatly appreciated. After every meeting my husband and I have with Tony over tea and cake, I always go home fired up with the enthusiasm to carry on writing. Tony is an extremely talented and accomplished author who writes under the name of Philip Yorke, and his best-selling novels are must-reads for lovers of historical fiction.

A big, big thank you also to my darling, long-suffering husband... What would I do without you?

And last, but not least, to 99-year-old 'Uncle' Jim, for the long phone call we had talking about his days as an SBA.

Other books by Emmaline Severn

GLORIA – From the snowy steps of Durham Register Office, Gloria is thrust into the life of an upper-class London doctor's wife, but haunted by a gypsy woman's prediction that she will never find true happiness, will her hasty marriage stand the test of time? A towery novel telling how Gloria's emotionally charged life shapes her transition from girl to woman. Even two world wars could not extinguish something so beautiful. A must-read and a friend you most definitely will return to again and again.

RICHARD THOMAS PARKER – As a family descendant, Emmaline writes a true account of the events leading up to the hanging of Richard Thomas Parker, the last man to be publicly hanged in Nottingham, on 10th August 1864, for the murder of his mother at Fiskerton, Nottinghamshire.

Also published by the author under the name **Catherine Pincott-Allen** with the **Field Detectives**

A FURTHER ACCOUNT OF THE HACKER FAMILY - This book is a focused research project on Colonel Francis Hacker's genealogy, primarily his direct ancestors and descendants during the 17th to early 18th century. It helps dispel some of the myths and legends surrounding their family tree. It also touches on the historical facts relating to Francis's involvement in the execution of King Charles I in 1649, which ultimately led to Francis's own execution on 19 October 1660.

www.ingramcontent.com/pod-product-compliance
Lightning Source LLC
Chambersburg PA
CBHW030536080526
44585CB00014B/965